"There is a satisfying notion of understatement in many of these well-wrought and intelligent poems [from *On The Ledger of Fruitful Exchange*], supporting the notion that Sirr is one of our most watchable younger poets." Fred Johnson, *Books Ireland*, 1996.

"Peter Sirr's desire to know his city [Dublin] means that it features in almost all the poems in *Bring Everything*, and becomes a character in its own right. Yet Sirr's city is usually inscrutable. When it offers itself as a poetic image the city seems to be deliberately avoiding taking on substance...Sirr becomes a *flâneur* of the new economy, traversing a place in which street names seem to have lost their resonance and where individual human stories of others are out of reach." Colin Graham, *The Irish Times*, January 20, 2000.

"*Bring Everything* in 2000 [...] is one of the best books of Irish poetry in the last ten years.... Ireland has undergone great social and cultural change in the last decade—economic improvement, increased immigration, openness to external influences—and something of the energy of these transformations [is felt in] Sirr's poetry. He has abandoned the nationalistic terms of reference of previous generations—stretching from the nineteenth century to poets such as Thomas Kinsella, Eavan Boland and Seamus Heaney—and is more preoccupied with the city as poetic arena." Justin Quinn, *Contemporary Poetry Review*, 2004.

"Even if it sounds pretentious to put it in these terms, Sirr's abiding and restlessly pursued subject is the components of a life: the things that make our life be what it is in particular. So in the brilliant and haunting poem "Hunting the Bricks and Mortar" from his much praised 1995 collection *From the Ledger of Fruitful Exchange*, the speaking voice goes foraging through the streets, finding a brick, flowers, the corner of a garden—all the things we recognize as the elements of someone's life. But the guidebook (his poems are full of books) fails to direct the speaker to the essence of a life, "the way... the light will strike a window" to form life's hearthstone. [...] In this search Sirr might be called a mystic of the ordinary. The ordinary makes this poetry sympathetic and appealing—even familiar—but the mystical makes it challenging." Bernard O'Donoghue, *The Irish Times*, April 23, 2005.

# SELECTED POEMS

# PETER SIRR

## SELECTED POEMS

Wake Forest University Press

Wake Forest University Press


First North American edition published 2005



Printed in the United States of America
Library of Congress Catalogue Number 2005927659
ISBN paperback 1-930630-22-0

First published in Ireland in 2005 by The Gallery Press
(Peter Fallon, Editor)

## *Contents*

*for Enda Wyley*

## *The King in the Forest*

Here a reign endures, among the trees,
someone's lordship of small noises —
leaf-tides and birdsong, a fleeing hare's
diminishing returns, and underfoot
the brittle politics of the forest floor.

Elsewhere battlement and parapet assert
our so much less than godly rights.
Prince of nothing, antic inheritor
of everything ungovernable
I venture deep into the forest . . .

Habitat of the hesitant, where shy
motions proliferate! Flowers proffer
nothing comprehensible, fungi observe
not the least heraldic rule, and the slender
deer elude me. I am a connoisseur

of ash-*lied* and oak-elegy, and when
the limbed light comes through the trees
I am the startled interloper set down
in a corner of the canvas, an afterthought
or a study in perspective, who sees

the leaves transfigured, the thin hands raised.

## *Guido Cavalcanti to his Father*

How will I know you where you lie
low among the dog-tagged
prisoners of iron and fire
or how, hearing only
the agreed text into which
their solitary cries cohere,
will I distinguish
your tiny paradigm of pain?

Nonetheless I draw near, borne
through special categories of despair
towards my own sins' region.
I bear to the unappeased
bulletins from the upper air,
impossible memories stowed
in a little fleet of images.
What do I hope to salvage here?

Yet I would stagger again up the beaches
of those flawed havens
where we who hardly dared collide
delicately improvised,
building trust like huts from driftwood;
I would endure again each silent storm,
words like provisions under sand
or maps of lands we strained to find

and each attempt at reparation
that proved a shyer kind of failure.
If they should find each other
let our eyes, like vying households,
at last abandon ruse and armour
having nothing now to lose
in this late kingdom, Father,
where no one hesitates.

## *Translations*

The strange fruits for which we have no name
are ripening in the nearest thing to heat;
hazy flocks flap close relations of the wing
and make the noise our language knows

as the rapid machine-gunfire of crickets,
hugely amplified, vivid concerti
for bin-lid and orchestra, the break for coffee
at a convention of electric drills.

Hard to believe our million
variants of light have never fallen here
or were not so quickly transformed
by what they fell on none was recognized;

to behold the lovely sketches published
immediately our mapmaker returned
and know in our hearts his hatchings lie
since everything here depends

on our having no way of expressing it,
on the wind blowing from a fifth direction
over the fabulous inland mountains
where clouds of yeti drift

and the shepherds are continuing students
of the idea of height;
on night arriving in a chaos of equivalents
as dreamed-of couples make furry love

on the plains, and nearby, in cartoon
houses, thickets aflame with claws,
the little family groups sit down
to divide the words for food.

## *Beached Whale*

Beached on the morning papers
you lie like a soft meteor
fallen from the sea.

All about you gulls explode
and crowds gather to record
your opulent decay.

The falsifying seas
may well have thrown you
out of orbit,

all your speeches bleak
monologues the waves distorted.
Maydaying hopelessly,

you went down like the sun
and dawn tumbled on the sand
your grey, gigantic death.

Now in your last resort
county councillors wonder
how to take you apart.

Somewhere there are simpler waters
and hours to reconstruct
the broken cries you broadcast.

And they will magnify you, the vast
assemblies of listening whales,
your throaty symphonies

brooding through dream oceans.

## *Lazarus Risen*

Lumbering out into the hectic light
like some dishevelled beast, I found myself
notorious, and would have turned back
but that cool and candid gaze unstitched
my shroud till it fell in shreds about me
and I walked among my weeping, bewildered kin.

Now their houses fall silent when I enter,
whey-faced and hesitant. For miles around
kids run howling home at the sound of my name
and when I pass even the trees look askance.
Sustained by a miracle, like flowers in a vase
my astonishing life continues in parenthesis.

Daily, strangers beat on my door.
How should I expect them to understand
my need for darkened rooms and blankets?
I still remember
Barabbas, drunk, circling the cross as blood
issued like a parable no one understood.

When they buried him I hid and waited
and saw his ragged body bleach the stones
and vanish. My arms hung like questions in the air.
They say my wits disdained that brusque choir
and smile at the familiar idiocy
that drives me now to watch in the evenings

the unearthly procession of light
from the grey loaves of the cemetery.
I think of silences broken only
by flesh loosening, the dry applause of bones,
while with growing confidence the spiky stars
transmit their small, post-dated fires.

## *The Collector's Marginalia*

The range is French and has a mind of its own.
All night long the turf crumbles in the air-tight
chamber and the hot ash rains on the tray,
yet morning finds the needle stuck at zero
and I come stumbling through the kitchen door,
the last of the true pioneers, arms laden
with firelighters and tins of beans, watching
through the window the smoke of a dozen
competent valley fires lean towards Maam.

After breakfast I follow the sunlight
round the room and copy out my phonemes.
I sit for hours in their homes, a casual
interloper listening for the square brackets
in the conversation, observing how
the troublesome genitive falls into disuse
in an afterglow of language. Looking up,
I see a trawler heading for the tiny pier,
the white foodmarket stark against the bay,

and wonder why I'm here, making coffins
for words. Yesterday I climbed awkwardly
to the top of the hill behind the house
past two famine cottages and an ageing
white mare looking down into the valley
like a receding myth, coming at last
to a pile of stones left for someone killed.
When I came down the fire had gone out . . .
On windy days I stay inside and watch

a lone tree grow sideways like something dreamed
or the idea of a tree, imperfectly grasped,
which the wind has brought from a country
where trees are possible. Each hopeful branch
migrates eastward to where the light falls

the right way up, in orchards, textbook meadows
or in slow encroaching shadows round hooded
monastery gardens where night shimmies down
the perfect canopies . . .

Out on the margins the serious stars
like drinkers gather, flashing sudden wit
above the huge, abandoned rocks,
the phone wires lying heavy on the poles.
My aerial's angled to the moon
as I prick my ears to the shaky news:
in three dialects the old people die
and the lights come on in local halls.
A volleyball team is making major strides.

## *Hospita*

Come here, you. Sit
down. For once in your life

simply listen.
Everything has been waiting:

the Chinese lantern
tilting like the earth,

the heirloom hoover
sickening in your hands,

that weight of delft
oppressing your deposit

till it cracks. Yours is the still life
the furniture edges

towards, the windows reach for.
True, the painter has died

who would have given this purpose,
who would have supplied

a hand to touch her,
eyes that held you

purely. But where have you been staying
that you have learned

to look so sheepish,
that you seem to have forgotten

nothing is yours
but the light you stand up in,

the earth yawning
under the carpet?

## *Colour Scheme*

*Red Bridges Cut Jump Risk*

— Newspaper headline

How could it not have occurred to them?
Could they not have seen
the colours were wrong? If they were here now
which of them would find it in his heart
to lie down before the lavender train
carrying its light load out of Oslo;
who could fail to smile at himself
watching the waves dance in the yellow estuary,
the hand grip in all seriousness
the dyed revolver? Released to look
again, what desolation could resist
the pulse quickening
over the gay street, the heart leaping
on the brightest bridge in Norway?

## *Some Things*

I need to believe I am hugging you
but the room leaps over your shoulder
hard and clear, as if you weren't enough
and faith kept coming back to this,
smoke veining thinly from your ashtray,
bare boards and chrysanthemums.
                                                    Look,
I hold you close, but draw in too
the table's clutter, the Matisse poster,
the billion hairs on your Shetland sweater
I'd almost count.
I am hopelessly involved
with the fly on your wall, the pouty blooms
revolving on your line. Two
storeys of a factory
are leaking through your window, half a stack
with its rag of sky . . . You
might be stealing through me, blind
to the world's intrusion, blind even
to my mind's idiot
hungering for consummation —
or you are locked in your own clear-eyed prison,
seeing your flat, as for the first time, and fighting back
its insomniac bric-à-brac.

## *Coming Back*

We know we have returned
when the first brick hits the train
flung in what must be ecstasy
from the embankment above
and the racegoers, outpacing us
since the Curragh with their lore,
unleash the fury
of their binoculars;

when our soft laughter mocks the city
on the bus ride in
and we can hardly keep
ourselves to ourselves.
A week away, and look,
the quays still lose their grip on history,
the river lifts and falls
in the memory of tourists . . .
Here we survive

crab-bones, shells, your gentle
*trouvailles*, the pansies
buttonholed in the sand-dunes
as a reproof of irony;
each aching journey home
to our old coastguard station
squatting on its hill
restored, half a century
past distress.

## *Already*

As if they had arrived already, displaced and harmless,
the grubby city, the (yes, again!)
dampness of the climate,
me there, sociable, abridged . . .
Yet as you remember us
in the long words of that country
think of me undoing every one,

breaking the compounds up to leave
only the simplest gestures,
flying ahead to destroy
the road in from the airport
where you become fluent again.
Think of me
drawing breath to divert

the young republic's ships
from the distant islands
whose one trouble-free legacy
you wash down with wine, sitting
with the friends I've kept my eye on,
seeing them stretch
across a year of envelopes.

Or admit me to the celebration
as a tang of *saté*
drifting from the kitchen,
as the hands of the Moluccan boy
who serves you,
let me enter
the language of your childhood

as a disruptive idiom,
a slow debate
on the futility of translation;

or waft across
to your attic flat
as flyleaf and epigraph, the first song sung
in the long tradition

though already we are talking
like the last pages, like our thinning letters —
your face across the single pillow
dying as I read,
my voice seeking out your bed
as a half avowal, an accent settling
between passion and composure —

already my fingers have begun
the long trek down your skin
as if they had imagined it,
as though it were the locked
flashback of an exile's mind,
a softness years since fixed
trembling for him still.

## *Postscript*

Could we ever live, you and I,
safe from the trashy grief
of airports, train stations
and last nights in borrowed flats?
The furniture is bored with emotion
and Karajan, too, has registered our intrusion
like a cough. Sibelius dies
in a wail of tannoy admonishments
and we are at the last barrier again
one flight-call from absence.
Do we love this,
the lightheaded return to the city,
the mournful, inventive gaiety
of our notes shuffling across Europe
wooing themselves?
I open your palm like a letter
in which little is risked; we hug and kiss
on the platform, dithering without a word
above the impulsive flourish of our lives.

## *Understanding Canada*

Tonight
he is understanding Canada
curled up under the standard lamp
with his thoughtful look, eyeing me
like a Whiteoak dreaming of Jalna
or wanting the music down
to explain about the Quebecois poet with the Irish name,
Ukrainians in the open spaces, nights trying to pick
between Greek Orthodox and Greek Catholic.
I have never been to Canada,
he has never crossed the Atlantic
though he sits sympathetically,
his mild gaze an open house
for the Iroquois, the Inuit, and later,
as if our hour had come,
he'll turn his head to mine and sigh
with a thin, migratory passion
the last words of our spoken language.

## *A Guide to Holland*

Audrey Hepburn moons big-eyed on the cover,
a shaded nipple just visible
under the woolly *O* of Holland,
and somewhere between *The Night-Watch* and
   *The Prodigal Son*
the inevitable
grim-faced matron is picking her way
down the stairs, clutching her High Nellie
as if her life depended on it, as it may,
while Father puffs his pipe in a well-lit room.
Land without secrets, heart worn
on the sleeve of Europe . . . near the zoo
a cardboard tiger aims his leap
at an apartment block, and here three months
I borrow the posture, sinking my teeth
into the interior life, matching
each flagrant privacy
with a dry French eye and an oath
for the commissioning editor;
letting the ancient rivalries begin,
the clever nation rescue itself again,
a smell of polders and *jenever*,
a chummy grin for Voltaire's 'infernal phlegm',
a pencil sharpened in a tall hotel
for a final assault on the bourgeois soul . . .

## *Expedition*

Refusing black, she wore the turquoise dress
he'd loved her in, straight, unbelted,
its wool strands curling towards the light
of countless photographs, nerve-ends straining
on Irish hills, a park in France, these woods
I hack my way through, blundering back
to high boots and bell bottoms, her face at twenty,
grieving foolishly
that so much of us lies like this,
beyond trespass, an album
of dangerous thrills closing
on an image still to be developed,
the print of her return, the soft
shock of the future
lifting with her dress . . .

## *The Nth Draft*

For weeks nothing had fitted.
I had been trying to remember
details, connections. Everything in my room
was unfinished, half-imagined,
and when I went out half the town
had crept away. The whole train journey
I stared out at an Atlantis
of dazed canals, power lines vanishing
above abrupt estates, trees rooted
in mid-air; trying to piece it together, that nagging
blur of cattle, the silhouetted
tractor, the village you could lose forever;
as if the whole country was an elegy
I couldn't conclude, acre after acre
gone stale. When I stepped out you were there
and I would have made something of that too,
I'd have had you walk on air, your body
a ghostly paraphernalia, your smile
weirdly decisive. Instead, you kissed me lightly
and led me through the streets, the fog
that stayed for days, or lifted that night, I forget.

## *Two*

### 1 fly

A bluebottle has buzzed in to settle
on my father's face. Why not here
as anywhere? It crawls on the greyed face
and hops and flits, filling the little room with its noise
which is like any other, the scratch of footsteps
on the sun-loosened tarmac
of the mortuary car park, the buried groan of traffic
through the open door. And we add ours, the darting
blankness of grief, a panicked cry
dying quickly in the city air, the Carmelite's
perfunctory stream of prayer, the fly of ritual
which touches everything and stays nowhere.

### 2 the machine

We had burst into the dream hospital
and opened the door, wanting to touch him.
And there it began, the body tied to nothing, gone,
with only the finally perfect machine
he had become, all light and chrome,
huge, bland, glistening and winking
with absolute purpose. Farther up,
where we should have arrived
like magi at the tented head, a screen flickered
and I saw my father move towards his own image
and dance gently into himself.

## *A Legacy*

When they lifted the pavement you could see
how the whole city rested dangerously
on sand or dirt or water
and how all three
would rise above themselves, staying
until they stung your sleep
or spoiled your newest rug.

You could never get away from this,
the graves set up above the ground,
the wooden piles
still making the news,
days you'd wake to the big drills,
the sound of footsteps
hurrying on the planks

and your own amazement
at how the earth had failed you,
your body
leaning acutely against the air,
his face
defeating history, risen
like the wrong coin and only inches from the street.

## *The Names of the Houses*

The village licks its fingers, belches, sighs, invites the yarn,
the childhood folly dragged up again and again
and as funny as ever. You know the pie has succeeded
in *Rustic Delight,* while over in *Well-Satisfied*
the prospective son-in-law has them eating out of his hand.
Architecture of content, profit all year round,
and the houses full of mirrors. And all looked down upon
by the bloated in heaven, the sated
belt-loosening forebears telling it like it was,
joy without end, flagrant happiness
with, maybe, in the off-limits backstreet, the smelling-to-
   high-heaven
shithole hovel of the village weirdo —
look at him now, the witless fool, slopping out
in *The Place of Violence, The Maiden's Ruin, The Life as*
   *Normal.*

## from *Here and There: A Notebook*

*Here* is a tight terrace
through whose thin walls
lives leak continually,
laughter and rows,
howl of petulant dogs,
my neighbour's piano
spilling daily into my head.
The street is narrow, the houses
so close, to glance out the window
is always to be met by eyes
glancing back. Humane horizons . . .
A Turkish family
lives opposite, the men serious
and dark-suited, the women in their
flowered dresses and headscarves.
How many generations?
How many children are there?
What is she thinking about,
the woman whose eye I catch,
smoking a cigarette by the window,
her elbow resting on the sill?
The men sit in bars so bare, so ugly
the natives hurry past, wondering at
that plantless brightness,
kitchen chairs on a wooden floor, a din
of maleness — strange islands
in a sea
of *gezelligheid*.
What do I know?
I've lived here a year
hermetically sealed
from the life of the street,
worrying about connections.
Yesterday, a week to Christmas,
a man I've never seen before

called with branches of catkin,
told me to put them in water,
then disappeared.
Last year, on New Year's Eve, at midnight
I stepped outside to watch
the fireworks. A door opened
across the street, the house
whose curtains are always drawn,
and a man came out, unshaven,
wearing an old string vest.
In his hand he held a revolver
which he fired twice into the air,
then he came and shook my hand
and went back in, smoke trailing
from the gun barrel.
His son keeps his Alfa Romeo
outside my window, sleek and black,
on the bonnet a huge transfer
of a wolf snarling. The man himself's
tattooed, forearms aglow
with sex and power.
I prick my skin
to let the pigment in
but little holds.
Again and again
the eye migrates, complains,
wherever it goes
is a city like this
undiscoverable,
in the dim suburbs of perception
a surfeit of detail.

# *The One Dim Thing*

See how he has turned to her, to that one spot
where her neck takes the light and whitens
to perfection; see how his finger strives to enter
that light and how, again, it is the same room, the same

heartbreaking light, the light of argument and desire,
the one illumination here: obsession's heaven,
the one dim thing relentlessly reached for,
the single gesture failing infinitely to accomplish itself.

He gives it up and settles back, he looks out the window
at the grey town: spires and rooftops, his own life creeping
like a burglar there. They lie absolutely still, the end of love
seeps through them like a drug, and because they are
 different

it works differently in each. She is drowsy now, almost
 asleep,
but his sceptical hands start out again, on their
ancient journey. They are not his hands now, they stray from
 him
like innocents, pilgrims who left the very hour

the faith shifted. Soon he will leave, or she will,
and his hands will come back to him, days later, or weeks,
in the final scene. Much has yet to be decided:
whose room, what town, what exact degree of passion, pain.

In the end nothing of this may remain,
neither the room nor them, not a limb, not a single hair —
though the light I capture is the light they've left
and every shot is bereft . . .

## *A Few Helpful Hints*

Tell them what you like. Tell them
the world is flat and when you get to the edge you fall
into the usual darkness, hell if you like
but anywhere will do, any storied space
mythical returners have whined of, salty
and smelling of loss. Tell them the rain falls
and steals slyly up and falls, and falls —
tell them everything twice for emphasis
and then again the next day for revision.
Set them tests on the same thing time and time again.
Tell them most of life is repetitive
and this will stand them in good stead.
Tell them about gravity and love,
drop the whole world on their heads
if you have to, the broad curriculum
of hatred and desire and the need for money
and love, tell them some things are permissible
and some less so, though ideally we'd prefer it
if you left that to us. Above all
don't be heavyhanded, keep a light tone,
encourage them to laugh, encourage them to believe
they are getting away with something when they do.
Encourage them to see you as a fragile,
merely human being. Forget things, mix up names
and be occasionally unfair in the allotment of marks.
Tell them about yourself if it helps.
Break down if you have to.
Tell them we could all be blown out of it
or the sun might go out or too much get through.
Tell them not to use aerosols, organize a project
on it. Projects are good. We like to stress
the need to work together. Harmony
is the oil in the machinery, or something
like that. Tell them about the men who came to save us
with beautiful voices and a poetry

we would like to have found time for, we may yet
retire to. Tell them about those
who have still to come, shuffling in awkwardness and anger
from the cardboard slums that tremble even now
on the outskirts, whose poems
may already be struggling in our blood
or hurtling through the dark cathedral spaces,
achieved and pure, unsettling the stars.

## *Through the Window*

As if, sickening of the view, you only had to look
far enough out the window, past
the serious shapes of the rooftops, the spires,
and find, somewhere off-centre, the harmless suburb
where the days wait like bandages
and the nights are a sweet coolness
and all of childhood simply this, a convalescence;
a white room waking into the same few sounds:
water running softly, sleep-happy voices,
the radio lapping the floor as you dress.

As if some part of the mind must always give up
and look for a smaller place, a pension
of painless perfections. My father, for example,
is always healthy here, his body young and trim
and always *moving*. I hear his knees cracking on the stair
like muffled gunfire as he comes to call me:
I see him running backwards, arms up,
face serious, catching the ball I've thrown
to test him, his safe hands seeming to grip the future,
his energy like a current arriving at

his own helpless body a decade later,
charging it somehow, and flowing on into mine
as I lift him up and help him walk.
I am dragging the past, healing us,
the boy throwing the ball who doesn't ask
for this, the hands lost in the simple act
of catching. Year after year I arrive here,
out of breath, and stretch my hands into the air
as if *this* were the image, and they had turned to me,
*Were you watching us? Did you see what we did?*

## *The Pursuit*

And if you were here there would be
that fury of touch, that drive to believe,
flesh raining on flesh till the whole
field flourished and I ached again
to bring you home. There would be
the usual fears and holdings back, the perpetual
sweated harvests borne uncertainly
yet also with joy. There would be
the high speed of language as we struggled to reach
the place where at last we could rest,
the pined-for slow resort where the mind
brakes and the language sleeps and we had
nothing to do but linger in the interim.
Instead of which I send, and not even to you,
but to something inside my head, the expected
speculative lyric, the flashlamp scouring
the cave of love and finding a spider-spray
of voices, ancient tangles flirting in the beam.
I have resorted to an old trick,
hymning the distance again, hoping to have you come
very slowly from there to here. Relentlessly I dream
of our arrival, a midpoint, some northern town
waking pristine in its dawn, and us there
anxious to begin, pursued by our old
offended selves, till we almost disappear,
living by hints, half things, tremblings,
blurred to each other in the retreating town,
in the fog that is our own breath
pulsed from fearful lungs, till finally
we've lost them — and become legendary —
the bill-posting, reward-offering, maddened
old ghost and all his underfed, regretful soldiery.

## from *Death of a Travel Writer*

### first ambition

To push through the cities
with the obstinate delicacy
of the blind tourist
who, in spite of you, knows his way,
who asks to be shown
everything, enjoys
your discomfiture. The cathedral, he says,
*The Last Supper*, the pigeons
anxious in the square.

Who will infinitely ignore
your blustering gifts:
the white stick, the faithful labrador,
the fumbled intersection
and the pavements raked
for pity. Who will touch nothing.
Who will give you back
his mythic fingers, his preternatural hearing
and go without memory or miracle

through the darkest streets.

## third and fourth ambitions

To bequeath, finally,
the white silence of myself
you would never have imagined
ached behind those words.
All that time I was rubbing
myself out. It took many volumes
to get this far. Oh how
I have had to labour
for my erasure!

To come back once more
but so lightly
nothing would mark the entrance,
not a leaf would quiver
or a single exhalation
be added to the air,
coming down in a freight of rain
with the silent messiahs
landing everywhere, wanting nothing.

# *Anatomy Lesson*

Pray for
Cornelius Magrath, Irish giant,
pictured here
dwarfing a Prussian grenadier,
his ambitious bones in glass
nearby, the bad gland secreting
death in poor light.
A wonder all his life
and after, his body stolen for dissection
packing the theatre
as his bones suck us here now
in the dusk chosen to light
medicine to art.
How much is possible,
the bones appeal,
the great pelvic spade,
the vast, deserted cage.

## *Cures*

For jaundice a stunned bat worn around the waist
until it dies for epilepsy glow-worms in a cloth
loosely tied, laid on the stomach
for deafness a lion's ear for melancholy an ostrich
for desire a sparrowhawk, camphor, *calandria*

For drunkenness a little bitch half drowned
her head rubbed against the veins
for dimness of the eyes a salve of apple leaves
for dropsy the spindle tree for migraine
aloe, myrrh, poppy oil and flour

For barrenness hazelnuts, convolvulus, water pepper
for baldness bear's grease, ashes of wheaten straw
for the heart storksbill, nutmeg, for the devil mulled copper
for vexation compress of aspen for catarrh tansy
for worms cherry seeds for fever tormentil, honey

Rowans plums sapphire emerald in wine
topaz in a ring to show poison for fleas dried earth
for hatred a doe for silence the sea for pride
alabaster, oak, leopard, the wrecked sun
creeping to its hut, the night hugging and hoarding

its secret alphabets . . .

# *Body and Soul*

Minced lamb, apricot jam, milky bread
while onions, garlic, ginger soften

not having forgotten bananas, bay leaves
nor neglected

two eggs beaten into the remaining milk
the whole to be baked, and served

on a bed of saffron rice
details available

in most good newsagents, the one
still open, the sad small place

selling also socks in piles of six
grey, navy, black, set down in a basket

near the cold shelves
where butter, milk, rashers, cheese

sit behind plastic veils,
the whole shop a shrine to the sustenance of desolation

oh purchasers of sombre socks and butter
the restless having woken

and hurried to the place, barefoot, breathless
pointing things out to the woman who sits behind the
  counter

in front of the cigarettes, beside the Lotto machine, near
the chocolate fingers; and exhausted walker home

from the faraway party, the minced lamb, the low flame
under the heavy pan, the garlic, the onions, the apricot

light, the milky grass, the lambs dancing in the planet's
craters, the women sleeping on beds of ginger

entering in a dream to buy
bangles, silks, apricot jam.

## *Recognition*

I had spread them out between us
so often our bed was like a map:
the heraldic crunch of the gravel path,
the pines going through their old routines
of boredom and sudden laughter

Now your car door slams in the drive
and I am
only a little surprised

My mother looks through the kitchen window,
years falling like the suds
she rinses from her hands,

and I can believe the familiar room
in which we turn and turn
as my body thins, as I grow
more awkward in your arms

I am retreating before your eyes

and this is the photograph you must take away,
the girl not quite fitting the clothes she wears
or your need to possess her,
whose wary eye you must return
like unlooked-for treasure to the bed we share:

in the morning we will struggle with the year, the day
the sky outside the window exactly
as I said it would be

and the bodies lying so close together
someone must surely break the silence
with a name, a gesture; someone must rise, easily,
into the known room, the recognition.

## *Listening to Bulgarian Music*

God grant me crooked corn and a cool day
she prayed, and it happened.
At the end, his family conceded defeat
and trudged home, lit by their own gold.

The field was all hers and she moved
down the outnumbering sheaves
to where he stood, his body bent
above the stubble, waiting for her.

## from *Pages Ripped from July*

### worlds

Landed, again,
in the infinite
fantasy of arrival:
the umpteenth door, the billionth stone,
the unbelievable thinness of the air . . .

Not that we had not
already left, nor that the fields
and endless mountains
had not long since foreseen
and ignored
our passing through them.

Where
are we now? There is
the sound of sea below the town,
there is the sound
of sandalled feet on old stone,
unplanned journeys,
the relaxed tread of good tyres.

Once this too
was the world. Now it lies
too far down, now it is sunlight
and finished history,
its deaths and blood
optional information.

We have
ourselves, we have
problems enough.
If you stayed long enough here
a door would open

you would not want to enter:
bearing your ordinary life

you would walk into the heat of the square,
the screams of the dying, the spectacle
of the already dead.
Carelessly you would be taken,
without any particular excitement,
and bundled onto the stone,
your blood, wholly unremarkable,
pouring into the sun
its brief stain.

## *Tenancies*

You float still
above the household,
your absence a live thing
which all our fingers touch differently
each recording its own shock

so that should you appear again
clamouring on the threshold
we would be the poorer
for the single undeniable gait,
the one

unmistakable voice
and the partitions coming down
of the house divided
into your separate tenancies;
for the poised

absolute body
glittering in our regard
in the one space left,
stitching the air between us
with a single thread.

## from *Home Ballads*

### 5 playground

You say
our lives are a school for the language of home

but it won't do. It's the not
being in I remember, need, the babble of interval

in which we huddle, far from the window.
Delicious, small atrocities

shake the ground before the bell's fury,
the single files. There is never

much time and there are always the faces
carried far, stern, kindly, not ours.

### 7 a lesson

You say
there is a language in which the word for family

is also the word for departure.
Handing across books, tapes, the world's

thinnest dictionary,
learn it, you say.

## *Trade Songs*

Taking from the West
eunuchs, female slaves, boys
also
brocade, castor, marten, swords

coming back with
camphor, cinnamon, aloes

this is the book of ways and kingdoms
the ledger of fruitful exchange

❖

Nine months in Vercelli
with the elephant Abulabaz
gift of the King of the Persians
to Charlemagne
brought by me, Isaac,
and wintered here.
It was late July
before the snows cleared
and we could make the crossing
another year
to bear the smiles of the Emperor
to Harun-ar-Rashid

❖

There is a town where they gather
having wandered off from the route:
the one place unchosen, the nowhere
happened on and stuck to forever

Ugly, nightmarish even, it has
this glory: that having come,

having bowed to nothing and witnessed nothing
and lived to tell it, no one leaves

❖

Coppersmiths, ironsmiths, porters, peasants
drawers of ships, dyemakers and, by royal command,
floggers and executioners

living all in a single street, their clothes ragged
recognized also by the red cloth
pinned to their breasts, the size of a gold coin

a valued and hated currency, a treasure buried
in 'the cesspit of the city'
where, fed and honoured, it pleased me to pass a year

❖

I see a little man dragging over a great space
a wagon filled with goods. Or it may be
gods he brings, who knows? Whatever it is
is heavy and his progress across what surface
has been imagined is slow. He travels like a stain:
first a spill, then a gradual seeping in
until he won't go away; there, he has stopped
pressed into the shirt of sand, grass dress
small but indelible. His stuff seeps with him
so that in the end they're all the same, a milestone
others navigate by, a monument to the world
as endless meal consumed by sloppy eaters.
By now, so much has spilled you can't tell
the garment from the stain. Noises from above,
laughter, someone crying 'More!'

It is heaven we hear maybe as we fall
on the soft cloth, weeping into the folds

❖

Others there were who had kept
a tenth of the laws and those badly

so that you might stay amongst them
a year or more and be taken

for the remotest stranger,
so that with misgiving you might enter

the house they call a temple
and be swept from it with anger.

Others to whom the light was offered
mistook it for the wrathful torch

and carrying its bearers to a public place
applied their error

❖

A little way out I saw them
gathered in the usual way,
everything done in the usual way
that obsessive diligence, that passionate
theatre of detail
that have never yet failed to make it.
Festival season, from town to town
the fire continues, lovers lie down
in celebration, ash like confetti
raining on their hair.

❖

Palaces by the water, places for prayer
port towns swelling
till the whole populace has a finger

in someone's eye, or

the once-in-a-lifetime deal, perpetuated
but never repeated. A night never to be forgotten,
the source of the fortune a throat drying

from fear and the effort of persuasion. It could have gone
the other way, it could all have ended with the razor
open on the table. The franchise came at dawn, the song

somewhat later. It was no harder than the others and it paid
for a year in Ravenna. I still walk through
doors it opened, celebrant

of the spirit of industry, sponsored and rewarded

❖

Our city was built on division, it is not so much architecture
as argument, each quarter brandishing its streets
like flags. You were loyal to your own skin

and you got out quick, and whoever offered you money
was fine by you. You wore the uniform of the king,
remembered not to ask his name, forgot your own

❖

Her eyes new minted
in the coinage of her city. My own
aspirant currency. Mulberry, woad, rice in fields

as dyked as Flanders. I took her by the hand
along the new canal, the law's latest arm
so that we all three trembled.

## *Hunting the Bricks and Mortar*

I have words, pictures,
I have my books on architecture —
splendours and duds, the brave
municipal dream, the dread hands
working up their own image
crying Look, O look, and in there,

in the thick of it, unbuilt
but not unimagined, my own
shelter, Home: hewn, dreamed,
timbered, stoned, set up and put upon,
mulled over, once begun, twice begun,
innumerable tearings down

and beginnings again. Through
the streets I go, foraging, lifting
a brick here, a gate there, one corner
of someone's garden, grasses, flowers
named somewhere: I have the book,
the notebook, I can hear the sound

they make, brick lowered upon
brick, stem upon stem and name
upon name: a litany, prayer,
a tiny burden to be taken
for safekeeping, for the hearthstone,
for the way, unreliably,

the light will strike a window
not there yet, not made,
not even gathered from the fire
but taking up the stubborn space between
one hand and the other, one finger
and the next, and carried everywhere.

## from *Pictures from a Glass House*

### a basket of broken glass

Prominent in a corner
the cullet-basket:
a basket of broken glass
waiting to enter the furnace again.
We touch glasses and taste the wine.
How far back
can our lips go? Think of it,
sipping the light of centuries
in a chain of breakage
all the way down
to this grey schoolbook picture

to William the Glassmaker
twice granted land
1258 and 1319.
Is that possible?
For years nothing is said,
beakers hang like bubbles in the air,
chalices catch fire and disappear.
Then, in a Castle ledger,
£5-13-6d
'wages for a glazier
working on divers occasions
and for divers colours
bought for making the glass windows
in said Castle'.

George Longe
kept his glass house
ten years in Drumfenning wood
or so he claimed.
He exported windows,
making the broad glass

by blowing the gather
to a long balloon
which could be split,
spread flat,
polished and cut
into small panes
*The windows are mine*
*so therefore the light*
*tumbling through them*
*on altar and aisle*
*Look ye keep it well.*

The forest is gone
that stretched from Dungarvan
all the way to Curryglass.

From Lorraine to Birr
came Abraham Bigo.
All his windows gone
his beakers extinct,
soda glass, green or brown
all of Dublin drank from . . .

❖

Still unbroken:
chandeliers, cruets,
baskets, claret-jugs,
epergnes and lanterns,
an amber finger-bowl,
pickle-jars, goblets
Lord Archbishop of Dvblin 1715,
*in pectore patria 1782*
Decanter, glass of lead
from William III

to Sir John Dillon
July 2 1690

❖

Bigo wraps a gather of glass
on the blow-pipe, firms it, trumpets
a soft bulb
which then is taken
on the rod they call
the pontil-rod
to the glassmaker's chair
not a chair but the bench
where the hot mix
is shaped, the stem added,
the mouth
pincered open: let it

cool in the cooling-oven,
let it fill and empty again and again,
let it fall on a hundred floors
in joy and argument;
let the glassmaker's servants
enter at a strange hour to harvest the fragments,
and bear them to where he waits,
impatient to begin, his lips
already moving for the tune;
let him blow and blow
till every beaker stumbles to our table
let our lips and fingers tremble,
touching every one, till touch turns to chime
and the hard skin begins to shine.

## from *A Journal*

*Lo sai: debbo riperderti e non posso . . .*
— Eugenio Montale, *Mottetti*, I

Hidden, misplaced, unrecognized
in the darkest corner of a dark house

you lie waiting for your time
the elsewhere my eyes return to

again and again to cry your name
like some scene in a film

of recognition, despair
or like the picture they returned today

to the famous hands that made it
after it lay for centuries

in the darkness of a smaller name.
How long have we been here

learning to love the shadows?
I come upon your body

believing, unbelieving, I hurt it into glare
wanting things to be clear

wanting to discover
if you'll blaze as fiercely there

❖

From Cornmarket to Back Lane
and back again, from Fishamble

to Marrowbone and Christchurch
to James's Gate, I look for it

the second city with its careless name
the half streets unstitching their stones
the markets shut and the lights turned down
Nobody moves or speaks

the cats have got our tongues and dream
their dark language, the bells are still
or pealing in your laughter
an epoch ends

in the roof of your mouth
and the rain idles in the clouds
waiting for us: but this
is too sweet

we need the nearer place
the rained grey
of the February street, the orange brick
of apartment blocks

rising fast, we need the sheen
of the developer's suit
the city in his voice
we need the rain to come straight down

on anxious afternoons
the black church to dog
the place of execution, the sky to surprise
the secret sign, the endless

hunger, the heart out
from Cornmarket to Back Lane

and back again, the cities spawning
Fishamble, Marrowbone, candlestick, tongue . . .

❖

In the beginning I went back to the rain
that had hung in the air for hours and finally came down
on the long road to the waterfall: it was a day of water
first the teasing sting of drizzle on our faces, the thickening
texture of our hair, then the gathering frown
and the accelerating shower swelling the ditches and the
stream
We could distinguish several kinds of watery sound
we almost wrote them down
in a book of rain, a journal of water
an almanac of matted curls and glazed hands
Rain on the roofs, rain on machines, the fury of drains
and the muffled resignation of piled wood
My anorak loud, your softening coat
and the growing thunder of the fall . . .
At the entrance we bought our tickets
watched the man return to his snug lodge and continued on
passed by a solitary car. It rained and rained
and the wetter we were the deeper we fell
Your hair shone to a gold I'd never seen before
your teeth glittered and your damp skin burned me to the
bone
We found a kiosk and stopped
for coffee, sandwiches, cake, all we could eat
as if the food might melt before us, the shop recede, leaving
only
the desolation of the picnic benches, the clattering rubbish
cans
the weeping *Fir* and the sad *Mná* listening all day
to the water roar. We followed the noise till we came to it

walking across the grass to the shining din
half its hundred feet obscured by its own spray
the driving rain and the crouched sky:
it fell in three great strands like fingers splayed
across the rocks and we leaned as close as we dared
past the danger sign, the No Climbing notice
You asked if we had a religion of water, if the site was sacred
and I saw the silent crowd, the water-priest shouting from
his rock
the children led to angry life or death. Houdini on his wire
honeymooners, desperate divers making sure . . .
The sky darkened, we walked slowly away
two days later you were gone again, the heaped engines
pouring: you climbed into the morning
and I went back to the rain-soaked bed, I leaned
like a maniac into the rocks until there was nothing left
but the ruinous crash
of water entering water, the madness of falling water

❖

What if
the language slips like water through our hands
there are
liquids more surprising

the heart raining
its thousand rains
the dreamed-of seas
gathering again

*Mare Tranquilitatis, Mare Nectaris*
sea of clouds and vapours . . .
slowly the valleys fill
and we go down

lifting heavy boots
like divers from Jules Verne,
listening for whales, moon-dolphins
flaring our names from the ocean of rains

the unknown sea, the sea of crises
and black desire . . . our light
blinds the shoals, our
signals fail, and unstoppably the waters rise

teeming across the surface . . .
look, the milky flood
dissolves the lines, stars drift
in the engulfing moon

❖

If I should be doing anything now
it should be that mute, folkloric thing
I should be sitting here stitching
a shirt for the loss of you
as the woman in the song I read
almost, but not quite, said
thinking of her long hours of misery
and solitude, her solitary misery
that set her thinking
of things she could make to dress the loss
the loneliness, making of the night
an infinite closet
to be walked through, full of hems
and rustlings, sleeved with promise
that fell to lace, eloquence, nothing
her death imagined then: a grim manufacture
of 'shirts for the sons of the grave —
stockings from great griefs

shirts from evil days'
till the place was awash with silk, linen
and Charon rowed fresh to dazzle the dead
to wrap them in shirts and lace
these shirts I borrow from the Finnish
this you left behind
to be wondered at, to be taken in hand
and hung again
or as if it might clothe
a lesser loss, absurd
these weeks I haven't seen, or heard
from you, this silence in which to dance
the darkest of our tangos
stately wilderness, my face
pressing yours to earth
the crazy, desperate thing

the heart achieves
on nights like this
planting the garden of the end of it
rising to a kind of hatred
to come back in, to come on spring
as a room surprised
by silk and linen, your lips open
your shirt undone . . .

❖

Not now, not yet
perhaps never
yet how slow this night is
with what infinite
patience it gathers us
sets us down
in the parallel avenues

streets of the unhurt
the absolved

brief, foolish: the lavender
stars, the moon in duplicate

big, stalled planet
where the hard things happen
and everyone survives
whose only literature
is the speculative fiction
in which my body turns to
and finds yours, in which

the mechanisms of departure
have yet to occur
I am telling you
I love you, I am mouthing
*Stay*, I have devised
an astounding machine
the rods and levers
clanking and turning even now
to articulate the possibility

## *Driving Home*

Eyes on the road, you tell me the legend
of your father's shirt on his neighbour's back
that it could be undone without shame
in the hospital. I see him driving home

like a ghost in his jacket, haunted by his own body
the wool chafed, speeding back to the kitchen fire
and a smile . . . his was the only car in the townland
and years later it lies in its field,

half bin, half shrine, its engine turning
in stories like this, coming to life
in my own hands as I speed
from windscreen to mirror, bearing to the future

chicken-wire, crates of empties
and the shift in which something loosened:
as the townlands flashed and vanished your voice
lightening, your face pressed further into the night

as your shirt unpeeled itself and floated off.

## *Sráid na gCaorach*

Ship Street deep
with the bells of two cathedrals

the day itself deepening
to that grey from which

suddenly, the city leans
as if it has remembered something

or woken again
to the wind on its face and the slow

geometry of light descending
and stretching towards them

with reluctance and strange joy
prepares to continue

a gull screeches over the castle
and Ship Street startled

rubs the wool from its eyes
and casts off . . .

## *China*

There's a moment the air will thicken and the light shift, as if
another country has poured itself in, another life
lent its corona      and suddenly the stars are here, milk spills
across the heavens; whoever you are ripples, splits, multiplies,
whatever there is flickers before your eyes
and if slowly the planet diminishes, if finally the ground
steadies under your feet and the spinning tongues resolve
into the one sentence in the one place, you'll still walk
with giant feet, still fall through the air, still speak
as if a shadow lengthened across the language

or it will happen like this:
a sudden, butchery odour on the street
and the pavement opens, the sky parts, something
floating back with such clarity it pulls you short:
an old early morning, your hand slipped back and falling
into your mother's, a few yards of strange brightness,
first a green shop, then a blue, a clock striking overhead
and then it's gone, then a blur, the rest of the journey
irrecoverable. What did it want? Nothing more than to say
this particular moment is on its own track, in its own time,
and if you should fall sideways into it, fall gladly

or you are staring out the window, going nowhere,
you are patrolling the gardens of China
and a shrub will open its bright door, a certain
aspect of gravel, a tender tilt of the planet —

Yet how foolish to have imagined otherwise, to have thought
our abandoned selves would not go on without us, quite
  unconcerned,
not to have noticed the small army marching beside us, on its
  way
to China, to Lipton's for groceries, to portal after portal.
We could be there now, loafing on stars, on a hammock

hung from days, watching the light
that lends us to the future and sometimes calls us back
and sometimes washes through us whatever it has touched,
  a drift
that settles in our bones, that tells us
we can no more live singly than light can fall on one place
  only.

## *Peter Street*

I'd grown almost to love this street,
each time I passed looking up
to pin my father's face to a window, feel myself

held in his gaze. Today there's a building site
where the hospital stood and I stop and stare
stupidly at the empty air, looking for him.

I'd almost pray some ache remain
like a flaw in the structure, something unappeasable
waiting in the fabric, between floors, in some

obstinate, secret room. A crane moves
delicately in the sky, in its own language.
Forget all that, I think as I pass, make it

a marvellous house; music should roam the corridors,
joy readily occur, St Valentine's
stubborn heart come floating from Whitefriar Street

to prevail, to undo injury, to lift my father from his bed,
let him climb down the dull red brick, effortlessly,
and run off with his life in his hands.

## from *Gospels*

Not, today,
the innards of machines and cities,
the rooms taken down and one by one

remembered, the ripped radio back revealing
the infinite tangle of things;
not even

how the rocket worked or the bird flew
on wings of detail;
not knowledge at all unless it be

hopeless, flaunting its one wing
in the empty library.
Things

magnificently vanish, sucked out of sight
till the day empties . . .
I'll stay a long time here,

erasure's emperor,
in the blown light of an endless room,
pulling the world back through itself

like a sleeve, leaving it there.

❖

Morning returns the world
We are gathered here
to refuse it

Having learned to sing the concealment
we have preferred to go on hiding
the light from the light

Can we now
ungather ourselves, think
of returning?

Small things, foolish
but the fork in my hand, the glass at my lips
and the water in my mouth

have not learned silence
Their language is everywhere
I walk among stone arguments

dust babble, the hubbub
of skin: my blood
chatters, my bones cry out

my eyes feed
on the noise of trees, my voice is a city
sunk in sand        I would

raise it again

## *Song*

*(after reading Leopardi's 'La vita solitaria')*

The stale town turns in dust,
dreaming hate;

a labourer leans out
and eyes the dawn.

With seeming joy,
in early rain
the cooped chicken
flaps its wings.

Look for me
in the galaxy of the stone,
in the ashes of the sun,

in the stubborn notes
of the servant's song
as she works through the night,
her voice filling
the empty rooms;

in the charity of the moon
above this town,
distinguishing equally
the assassin's knife,
the solitary life;

in all
that is pitiless and beautiful;

where earth meets water and water light;

where hope lies quiet
in the grave of things,
an undersong;

in the held breath of noon
look for me:
the world's aftermath
or second thought

when lake and sky and silence imagine
how it might be done;

in the eyes of the labourer at dawn
before the town has stirred
its ruinous dust,
the farmyard lightening,

and strangely joyful
in early rain
the cooped chicken
stirring, bustling its important wings.

## *The Beautiful Engines*

Seeing at last into the heart of things,
I could have stayed all day
hunched over a milkshake in the burger bar
watching the doorstop grip the door, marvelling

at all that came together there: the inclined plane in action,
the upward and the downward pressure, the friction
holding the wedge to the floor.

I was trying to be exact, I was trying to lean
a little farther in.
The children's book I bought today
tells me how things work: the lock, the key, the plough, the
  hoover.

There's a page
for the city splayed before me like a toy,
full of holes and the brightly coloured engines
which make, then fill, the holes

as there must be, flapping in my skull,
for the king eider seen off Brow Head, the scarlet rosefinch
  on Rockabill,
Baird's sandpiper seen last evening in Ballycotton

flocking in daily error to my computer,
fluttering their names as I log on,
with dates and times, with exact locations,
colliding with each other,

with the fridge churning in the kitchen,
with the water pistol, the dishwasher, the fire extinguisher,
with Des and Margaret, flown home from Cyprus

to wagtails on the north slob,
annnouncing their engagement en route, with my face
pressed close to the book
as if something might fly out from it

it would have been terrible to miss:
an engine released at last from its name
to flicker like lightning in the brain,
the valves of the planet looming through glass . . .

## *After a Day in the History of the City*

What vagabond bones
and you, too, Ivar the Boneless,
come together now
stench of what plagues
thriving again
and everywhere one turns
places of execution

Who should not prefer
to cross the river
and walk in procession
down the aisle of his own cathedral
with Samuel
Metropolitan of Oxmantown
wanting nothing from him but his title

or to say with Peter Lewis, cathedral proctor
Today came with his men Tady the hellier
to renew the slates
after the heavy snows of Christmas and the frost

## *Cathedral*

I dyd byllyd and pyllyd with oke timber
I fyllyd hit the foundacion with roche lyme
The masons paid, the carters paid,
the smith, the cooper, the casters of sand.

What I really wanted was to stand
for once empty-handed
by the vanishing spires and the bells
beautifully dumb, pealing quiet

as we waited, the world rinsed out of us.
Stone by stone the city returned,
these streets mapped by desire
the light that seemed to flare

from our own skin to press
the district towards us.
As if in a small rain of touch
we stood, and watched it grow.

I leaned towards you, provoking
a dark bricked brewery palazzo
you kissed me and caused
black tramlines to loop and veer.

When you stopped, they disappeared.
So greedy the desire
the whole place seemed to fall
and my spirit, that had been light, was air.

## *Legacies*

You so love company
an engine has attached itself to your body,
taking up the night and feeding it back
as a spill of laughter
and confusion.
It takes half of what you say
and chews it up, the rest it overlays
with heavy rock, with old films,
the roar of other voices, glasses
clinking and a till slamming,
someone arguing and someone
starting to sing.
But you don't mind,
it comes with the grammar
in this dialect of intimacy,
it's how you like to live at night.
It's where your father lived
and his father before him;
it has poured down the generations,
loud and smoke-filled,
a background roar where the soul
grins; it is the city
refusing to sleep, talking to itself,
drinking too much.
What happens here would die in quiet,
melts at dawn, is absent from
the sensible rooms our friends
have retired to. They've gone
to sleep or talk, to use the language rationally,
to distinguish one sound from another:
the purr of far-off traffic, the hum
of heating and the gravity of early news.
We're listening in the nth bar
to your great great grandfather
blurt his song, to his son urge him on,

then *his* son comes shambling in
to wave your hands and shout for more
in your voice: more talk,
more drink, more noise
till neither they nor you nor I can tell
whose head is starting to spin,
whose voice is telling the story,
whose life it happens in.

## *Hunger*

1

Right here, right now
on the lavender sack
by the olive trays

a scoop of olives
for your mouth
and goat's cheese for your thighs

let me
lie down with you
in the havoc of the market . . .

2

Because you gust through the room
making things occur,

the fruit to fly from the fruit bowl
and the furniture to quail,

because the olives are all over
and the meal

may never recover,
tonight's outpost

of the empire of laughter
invents a ceremony:

the orange touch, the olive kiss,
the lying down, it seemed forever,

in juiced rain and lavender storm

3

Cry Hunger, Hunger
silencing the vendors, causing

the buyers to stare. Such
havocs of tenderness

wreak there
spices will fly, lavender rain

on the city,
the sky grey with November,

the heart with old anger.
With tang, with colour

baffle them, bless them,
and the sound of laughter.

## *Housesitting*

This is a life, and I move
towards it, the aisles
crammed with pet food
the cliffs with substantial houses
angled to receive
the narcotic sweep of bay
A painted sailor looks seaward from a lawn
in an attitude of readiness
A hand reaches from the dreamlife of the town
to pat him on the head
In the new economy
a man leans to me in the hill-top park
to tell me the price of a house below
and abruptly goes
Who, ever, is at home in a life?
The dog claws the wall and strains over
I stare for hours at water
an infinitely concentrated carelessness
begins there
in which I may be learning
to lend myself to myself
to lodge and withdraw like the sea
or be the beach ignorant of its own account
On my sleeve
a labrador's heart
See how fiercely she has laboured this large stick
all the way home, so that I can hardly walk beside her
Joy, fear, hunger
grip, then leave
I sleep
on a landing close to myself and wake
to my own breath, listen, stirring
beyond the door

## *Desire*

Reconstruct me from a closing bookshop,
from the panic of shelves
where old cars trick the spirit, manuals
of self-repair; gods, geography, money

and little time. Sniff the air in poetry,
lay a blanket down and wait
where a furious concentration hunches over
Teach Yourself Amharic, Aramaic:

there's hardly time to say hello, hardly
a hair's breadth of the language to take away;
enough to be silent in, enough to watch
the insistent dust-mote

grow its mountain, the dromedaries
appear. Someone is arguing
in Old Norse, the sun wakes up in Persian
and I am walking out

with grains of light, pyramid crumbs.
Elsewhere, in the desert, in the hilltop village,
on an endless, meandering train
the soul puts down its books, fluent again.

## *From the Sunken Kingdom*

The lost continent moves towards us.
Atlantis, Atlantis
we have searched so long.
Mountains dissolve, a great lake opens, the sky
is a blue astonishment. The voice says
Go to it, settle on it, push
the heavy doors. Dust greets us, cobwebs, spectral linen.
Nonetheless we enter, nonetheless lie down.
The ropes are loosed, the drift begins, the mountains
are dark above us. A long journey, the land
aching beneath us. Are we moving still?
We look up at the lost stars, try to count them, try
to rope them in. Beyond them, the far peoples
stirring faintly, waiting for us to return
with leaves, promises. *The world is safe again, open*
*the doors*. They stand there, listening,
their hands heavy with keys
as many and as ancient as our own.

## *Unbuilt*

On my wall a print
of St Werburgh's Church,
white stone, solid spire —
too solid, as it happened,

too near the castle
for comfort, and so proscribed.
Nearby a dreamed-of street
comes out to play,

a giant cathedral
dips its toes in the river.
Monuments in every drawer:
the winged horses, the swords,

the upraised hands infinitely
persuading. Trams glitter among the trees,
their lacy, longed-for shelters
adorn the quays

and near the harbour,
in pavement cafés, their eyes shining,
the architects stay up all night
marching cities across a table.

In basement archives, patiently
the future carves its name,
the perfect avenues bide their time
just as, round every corner,

our own better lives catch fire.
Every now and then
we stumble on the plans
and marvel . . . Meanwhile, though,

there's this
dirt, mess, handsomeness,
the crooked streets persisting,
the sawn-off churches

keeping their peace, a grittiness
in the air like the breath
of the imagined, our
unfinished hearts

still building . . .

## *The Writer's Studio*

*(after the Francis Bacon Studio in the Municipal Gallery, Dublin)*

They've been worrying for ages
how best to show your chaos.
Two days from the opening
a curator rearranges papers,
spills ink on the floor, half-eats an apple
and throws it in a corner, but still
the disorder comes to order;
the flung pipe, the forgotten shirt
sculpted and composed, with the notebooks,
the scrawled-on walls and mildewed postcards.
It's all there, through the peephole,
this reconstruction of your mind
from which you are entirely absent.
You're in heaven cursing the dullness of angels,
throwing your clothes around like clouds,
prowling the fragrant avenues
for a fight, a drink, someone to talk to
or sleep with, and if some freak wind
planted you here among your own things,
you'd sweep the lot from under our eyes,
tear it all down, rip the postcards, the T-shirts,
rob the till and drink it dry and float
back up to your high bed and wake up
having forgotten everything. We
who so loved your life we made a fetish of it
will stand in the air, hoping to catch
whatever falls: broken crockery, a smashed cloud,
we'll see your hand in the wind and rain,
hear your voice in the roaring streets,
follow you from porn shop to pub
and back again. And then a tree will fall,
or a leaf, someone lean out a window,

a cat slope
down a laneway
and
at last
we will understand you.

## *In the Graveyard*

They lived and died in the same place.
The same names occurring, same big skies above.
This close, they must move still in their cottages
and walk their fields, or stand now watching
the mountains purpling in the last sun
and hear the sea turning onto the slope of the beach
its calm, insistent weight. The air's crowded with them
as they move and watch and listen, no one
having told them otherwise. And if
absentmindedly they drift back here
to this silent field, they'll find
the gate locked before them and their names
unreadable on the stones. They'll walk back towards the
   village
and climb into their beds, whatever was theirs still theirs.

## from *Office Hours*

The workers disappear into their buildings,
the work itself falls through the air,
sinks into corners, remembers itself.
A notebook wakes up in a drawer;
in a forgotten diary, under mounds of clutter,
the umpteenth PAYE week of the year

is drawing to a close
as early lunch floats up from the restaurant
and rain pummels the fire escape.
Today's rain, last year's rain . . .
the door opens
and someone lumbers in

drenched in eighteenth-century rain,
the rain of the great squares, Luke Gardiner's rain,
the Earl of Drogheda's rain;
stands there shaking the rain from his cloak,
wanting his lunch,
then crosses the chessboard flagstones

and approaches us, a large, fretful
impatient gust.
But we're impatient too
and walk through him as through our own
scurrying selves that come towards us
with their stacks of paper and unmissable deadlines

and maybe one of them will stumble,
lift his head, stall
long enough to stare out a window
and sing our lost labours
in rooms for the never completed,
for the ongoing review, the unfinished application,

the meeting still searching for a conclusion.
The delicate letter weighs up its options,
the fax we have been waiting for
is coming through, the fax machine itself
is on the way
and though the diary's run out

and the taxes are paid
our working lives continue
in their own time, the cables are laid, the calls
are put through to our desks again,
our hands fallen into the air
nonetheless persist . . .